MAORI MYTH

MAORI MYTH

THE SUPERNATURAL WORLD OF THE MAORI

illustrated by
Roger Hart

with text by
A.W. Reed

.H. & A.W. REED   WELLINGTON SYDNEY LONDON

First published 1977
A. H. & A. W. Reed Ltd
65-67 Taranaki Street, Wellington
53 Myoora Road, Terrey Hills, Sydney 2084
11 Southampton Row, London WC1B 5HA
also
16 Beresford Street, Auckland
165 Cashel Street, Christchurch.

© 1977 Roger Hart and A. W. Reed

All rights reserved. No part of this publication may be reproduced, stored in a retrieval system or transmitted in any form or by means, electronic, mechanical, photocopying recording or otherwise, without the prior written permission of the copyright owner.

ISBN: 0 589 01019 0

Typeset by N.Z. Consolidated Press Ltd., Auckland.
Printed by Kyodo Printing Co. Ltd., Tokyo.

CONTENTS

	PAGE
Introduction	6
1 The Coming of Knowledge	9
2 The Coming of Life	13
3 The Coming of Death	16
4 The Realm of Death	19
5 Tribal Gods	23
6 Enchantment	29
7 Symbol of Fertility	31
8 Media of the Gods	35
9 Denizens of the Forest	40
10 Denizens of the Sea	43
11 Denizens of River and Lake	46
12 The Coming of Pounamu	50
13 The Coming of Kumara	54
14 Witches and Warlocks	58
Glossary	63

INTRODUCTION

In his introduction to the companion volume, *Maori Legends*, the artist Roger Hart referred to the fact that Maori folklore was greatly influenced by the characteristics of the New Zealand landscape. His imaginative paintings gave evidence of a kindred spirit with the old-time Maori, and sympathetic understanding of their physical environment. Allied to this was some exploration of the depths of Maori thought. The double influence of landscape and the spiritual inheritance of Polynesian forbears is again apparent in the present collection of paintings, which is certain to be welcomed by admirers of his earlier work.

Source material is embarrassing in its richness and variety. In fact, it is a matter of regret that so little can be included in a small volume. Exciting epics such as the Maui and Tawhaki cycles of legends are conspicuous by their absence, even though many of the tales could be chosen to illustrate the theme. Emphasis has here been placed on the mystical and esoteric element in Maori rather than on hero stories, the major features of creation, or localised folklore.

Natural and supernatural phenomena are interwoven in the several aspects of Maori culture, not only in myth, legend, and incantation, but also in song and dance. Those who are familier with the myths of Polynesia will be aware that the Maori of New Zealand was fortunate in his heritage of gods. But he was also an individualist, even radical in his views. Tradition was sacred but not immutable. While their departmental gods retained the names and functions ascribed to them by their Polynesian ancestors their relative importance was changed, and for valid reasons. Living on smaller islands than their New Zealand descendants (in some cases even on atolls) the sea was all important to the Pacific Islanders as the source of food and therefore of life. Tangaroa, the god of the sea, naturally became the most important of their departmental gods.

Although no part of New Zealand is more than a hundred and thirty kilometres from the sea the land area was far greater than the largest Polynesian island group. Forested hills and plains provided birds, vegetable food, and eels and fish in greater profusion and variety than the sea. As the guardian of trees and, by inference, of all terrestrial phenomena, Tane therefore became the foremost departmental god of the Maori; the benefactor of the Maori people, the progenitor of life itself. As the ocean waves battered the shore, the supernatural guardians were naturally at enmity with each other and jointly against Tawhiri-matea, the god of wind, whose allegiance was with the Sky Father rather than with the Earth Mother.

These were noble, wide-ranging concepts. Dependence on the supernatural representatives of life-sustaining forces is nowhere more clearly exemplified than in the elevation of Haumia-tiketike, the guardian of the humble but necessary bracken rhizome, to departmental rank along with his more flamboyant brethren. There is also significance in the fact that Tu-matauenga, the god of mankind, was the undisputed victor in the first war of the gods, demonstrating the final superiority of the human race.

The most cursory study of Polynesian myths reveals superior concepts of the Maori. In addition to the pantheon of gods and their primal parents, Earth and Sky, the various aspects of nature were explained by countless personifications. Local gods, or atua, defended those who were subject to their whims, provided they were encouraged with correct and appropriate incantations. Tipua or enchanted objects abounded in lake, river, and forest. Above all, the hierarchy of heaven and chiefs and common men was bound by strict rules of tapu which stemmed from man's relation to the non-material forces of life.

It is these aspects of the inner life of the Maori that are here portrayed in picture and text (to the neglect perhaps of the larger canvas of fabulous and semi-historical legend). A number of legends illustrative of deeper themes are also included. To the artist the writer wishes to express his deep gratitude for his revealing interpretation of the dynamic forces that in the past have shaped Maori thought and are still evident in the contribution that should be and is being made to the evolving culture of the two races now known as New Zealanders.

The text of the present book leans heavily upon another volume by the same writer, *Treasury of Maori Folklore*, which explores the beliefs of the Maori in greater depth.

THE COMING OF KNOWLEDGE

THE TASK OF PASSING sacred lore from one generation to another was entrusted to the tohunga ahurewa, the medium of the gods. He was the expert in makutu (witchcraft), tapu (sacerdotal restrictions), and karakia (incantations). The root of the term tohunga is "tohu", meaning "to guide". The tohunga was responsible for passing on the knowledge he had gained from his predecessors and was required to practise it throughout his active life.

The school at which tohunga were trained was the whare wananga (house of occult knowledge). There were several grades, the highest of which was the whare kura (school of learning) in which historical traditions, legends, and the ritual of war and agriculture, as well as the deeper mysteries of their craft, were taught. In a metaphysical sense sacred knowledge was enshrined in stones known as whatukura and which were contained in the "baskets of knowledge". There were three baskets, containing the kete-aronui, the sum of beneficial knowledge, the kete-tuauri, the full range of ritual and incantation, and the kete-tuatea, the knowledge of evil and black magic.

The three baskets were brought from the overworlds to earth by the god Tane. During the nineteenth century the basic account of Tane's bold sortie into the overworlds may have been influenced by Christian concepts of good and evil, as personified in Tane and Whiro. It is reasonably certain, however, that Tane, who was the Prometheus of the Maori, was responsible for obtaining this gift to mankind at great risk to himself.

Tane was not the only god who aspired to obtain the priceless gift but after much dissension and chicanery Tane was the one chosen to ascend the overworlds in quest of the sacred lore. He had the foresight to select a suitable site for the first earthly whare kura in which the baskets were to be enshrined.

He then ascended to Rangi-tamaku, the second overworld, where he found a pattern for the whare wananga, which he copied on his return to earth. Tane ascended on the swaying ropes that were the rising whirlwinds of Tawhiri-matea. Whiro, who also aspired to the honour, followed his brother by a more circuitous route along the fringes of the several overworlds. On his arrival at Rangi-tamaku he learnt that Tane was in the next overworld and sent his "hordes" to attack him. It was a combined operation of mosquitoes, sandflies, owls, bats, and other nocturnal creatures. It would have

gone badly with Tane if Tawhiri-matea's whirlwinds had not scattered them to the far corners of heaven.

It is not clear how far Tane had to travel to reach the baskets and the stones in which the sacred knowledge was enshrined. One account says that he reached the tenth overworld where he engaged in purificatory rites. In the eleventh overworld he proceeded to Pu-motomoto, the gateway to the topmost heaven, where he was met by Rehua, the god of kindness, with whom he was well acquainted, and was presented with the coveted baskets.

In the meantime Whiro had been toiling slowly and painfully up the storeys of the sky. With his followers he lay in wait for Tane in the ninth heaven. A great battle ensued. The result was in doubt for some time but, strengthened by the knowledge he had gained in the ultimate overworld, Tane finally overcame Whiro and his hordes. They were driven down to earth where they made their permanent home. As a result mankind is constantly plagued by many of Whiro's followers.

Whiro himself was hurled headlong into the nether world where sickness, evil thoughts, and death are his gifts to men. He continues to father the Maiki-nui and Maiki-roa—the great and long-continuing misfortunes of mankind.

Tane, jubilant after his great accomplishment, left the overworld and entered the earthly whare kura, where he suspended the baskets with their precious freight from the rafters. The mana of the first of these stones, the Whatukura-a-Tangaroa, was subsequently conveyed to other stories in the many whare kura of Aotearoa, where they were used to seal the teaching of the tohunga, impressing the teaching on the minds of their pupils and adding mana to the recipients.

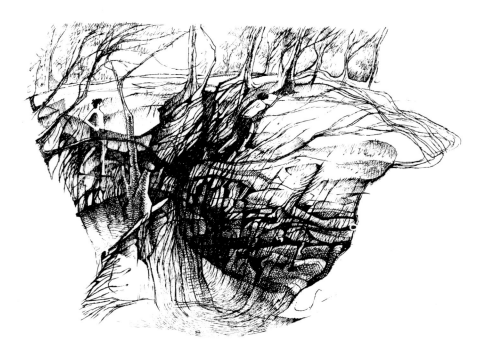

THE COMING OF LIFE

ALTHOUGH ONE OF THE youngest gods, Tane occupied an important place in the pantheon of deities. He was the life-giver, the fertiliser, the sustainer, the god of the forest and indeed of the whole world of nature, and the active element in all earthly life, as well as the bringer of knowledge. Among his descriptive names were Tane-mahuta, the source of trees, and Tane-mataahi, the creator of birds.

Apart from his feat in bringing the wananga to earth Tane's greatest accomplishment was his successful quest for the female element. The children of Papa and Rangi*, the primal parents of earth and sky, were all male gods, instinct with the ira atua (divine element), and were incapable of producing the ira tangata (human element) which could only emerge from the uha (female element). In Tane's attempts to find the uha and create mortal life he bequeathed many gifts by which mankind has benefited. His mother Papa had advised him to visit Mumu-hango, an already existent female personification and by mating with her he produced a variety of trees, birds, and insects. The union of Tane and other personifications resulted in a wide variety of natural phenomena such as stones, flood waters, muddy pools and monster reptiles. Two of their offspring in turn produced lizards, rocks, sandstone, gravel, and stone. But still a female element was missing.

After failing to achieve his purpose Tane returned to Papa who gave him the secret he needed. "Try the earth at Kurawaka," she said, "for in that place the female is in a state of virginity and potentiality. She is tapu, for she contains the seed of the likeness of man."

By this time Tane was in despair. "Old lady," he said, "there will never be any progeny for me." (This was surely the understatement of all time!)

"Go. Go to Ocean who is grumbling there in the distance. When you reach the beach at Kurawaka gather up the earth in human form," the Earth Mother insisted.

---

* The myth of Tane's separation of Papa the Earth Mother and Rangi the Sky Father and their subsequent adornment is related in *Maori Legends*

Reluctantly Tane took her advice. On arrival at Kurawaka he fashioned an image of earth, to be the first woman, Hine-ahu-one, assisted by his brother gods. The older ones were responsible for shaping the body while the younger ones added the fat, muscles, and blood. Tane the fertiliser then lay on the new-formed body and put the breath of life into its mouth, nostrils, and ears. The eyelids opened, the eyes lit up, breath came from the nostrils, and the living body sneezed.

The mating of the first woman with a god resulted in the birth of a daughter, Hine-i-tauira (Pattern Girl). Later children of Hine-ahu-one included personifications of hot springs, clouds, and lightning.

The offspring of Tane and Hine-ahu-one were all girls. Although motherhood and fertility are essential to the propagation of human life, the generative power of men was of equal importance. In spite of the fact that there are many different accounts of the creation of man it is doubtful whether such legends were ever part of the wananga, the teaching of the houses of learning. This in turn may account for the homely folktales that centre round the creation of Tiki, the first man. In one of them the progenitor is Tu-matauenga, the god of war, who represents upstanding man.

In one of the earliest accounts, the male element was of greater antiquity than the female, predating the separation of Rangi and Papa. Apparently a primitive form of vegetation was in existence prior to the separation, as well as an abundance of reddish water, and it was the combination of water and vegetation that is said to be responsible for the spontaneous generation of Tiki. His wife, Ma-rikoriko, originated by a more involved process. She was formed by Arohirohi (mirage) and Pa-oro (echo)—perhaps a commentary on the Maori concept of womanhood! When their grand-daughter was born clouds floated in the sky, water flowed, and dry land rose above the floods. Earth could be seen in the first light of dawn, which turned to full day when Tane lifted Rangi from the embrace of Papa.

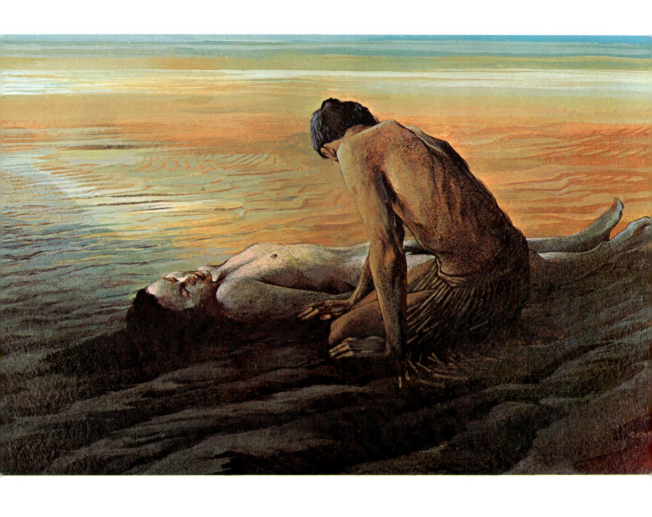

THE COMING OF DEATH

As TANE SOWED THE seeds of life in the Ao-marama, the world of light, so he was ultimately responsible for death, which comes sometimes with heart-rending sorrow, sometimes as a blessing, as during the sleep of the aged.

When his daughter Hine-i-tauira, or as she was so aptly named, Hine-titama (Girl of the Dawn) grew to womanhood, Tane took her to wife. Their first-born was the personified form of vegetable growth. When Hine-titama plied her husband with questions about her parents Tane was evasive and referred her to the posts of her mother's house which, he assured her, would reveal the identity of her father. The young woman was so persistent that at last Tane was forced to tell her the truth.

Saddened and disillusioned, Hine-titama determined to leave home.

"Where will you go?" Tane asked. "My presence is everywhere in this world of light. You cannot escape me."

"I shall not remain in your world of light," she said scornfully. "My grandmother Papa will shelter me in the depths of her body. The path of Taheke-roa to the underworld shall be laid down for all time. From the Muri-wai-roa I shall look up to you and our offspring moving in the world."

Her final words were prophetic. "Remain, O Tane, to pull up our offspring to day, while I go below to drag them down to night."

Tane protested, but Hine-titama was adamant. She chanted a sleep-inducing spell. Her parting gift to her father-husband was the Adam's apple which she placed in his throat as a token of their relationship. When quietness fell on the world of light, she descended through the space between the earth and the underworld. Ku-watawata, the guardian of the gates of the lower regions, attempted to dissuade her from going further but she remained firm, explaining that her purpose in going to the realms below was to protect her children of the upper world.

"Let me remain," she said, "that I may catch the living spirits of my descendants from the Ao-marama."

When she took her place in the world of shadows her name was changed to Hine-nui-te-po, the Great Lady of Night or Death. She became the goddess

of death, but is also remembered as a young woman fleeing from her shame, yet imbued with love for her innocent offspring and their descendants. In the legend of Maui the demi-god and his attempted conquest of death, she is represented as the dread figure of night swallowing mankind but in the creation legends she is a pathetic and yet beneficent personage, devoted to the welfare of her children. It was not her wish, but the consequence of her incestuous relationship with Tane, that brought death into the world.

Although she was the first to tread the path to Rarohenga, the world beneath the world, she is there to welcome her children. The body of man perishes and decays, leaving its spirit free to go to Rarohenga, to the sunny girl of the dawn, who, through the evil that befell her, has become the last refuge of night and the mother of death. Tane-matua remains as the protector of men in life, Hine-nui-te-po the guardian of their spirits in death.

The boundary between life and death is at Cape Reinga, the extreme northwest point of the North Island. On its rocky promontory grew an ancient pohutukawa tree, the branches of which provided a ladder for the spirits to descend through the swirling waters to the fabulous land below. Although some legends contain contradictory information it was not necessarily a place of shadow and sorrow, even though the departing wairua or spirit might be greeted by the mihi-tangata, the wailing of the innumerable dead. The wairua crossed the last river with the assistance of Rohe, the ferrywoman, and ate the food of the underworld.

There are several legends of visits by living men and women who have come to rescue loved ones from a premature death, but once food was eaten in the realm of Hine-nui-te-po there was no return.

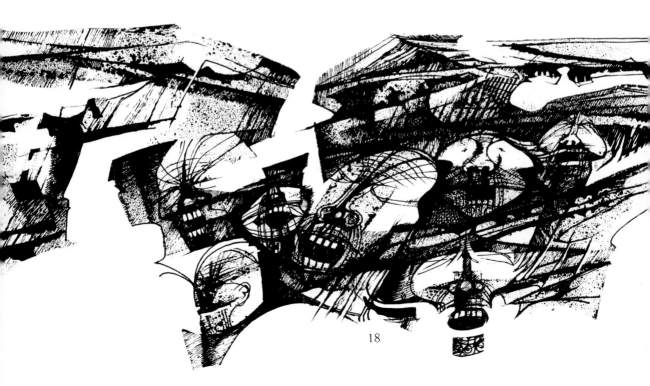

THE REALM OF DEATH

COLLECTIVELY THE UNDERWORLDS were known as Papa, the Earth Mother, just as the overworlds were Rangi, the Sky Father. The first of the ten planes of this former, mysterious, ill-defined region is the world we know, the world that was clothed with vegetation by Tane-mahuta. The second, the top layer of soil, is the home of Rongo-ma-tane and Haumia-tiketike, the gods of cultivated and uncultivated food. Then came Te Reinga, the leaping place of spirits, and Au-toia, where Hine-nui-te-po reigns. The fourth subterranean land is the realm where Whiro took refuge after his contest with Tane.

The next three were Uranga-o-te-ra, Hiku-toia, and Pou-turi. These three regions were controlled by Rohe who in life was the wife of the demi-god Maui.

Miru, the dreaded goddess of ultimate extinction, is the controller of the lowest three planes. The eighth region, which is her home, is unnamed. The ninth is Toki (worm), the tenth Meto (extinction).

It is not to be thought that these concepts were known to everyone. In fact an eminent tohunga who lived in the South Island in the early years of the present century maintained that the ten underworlds were a corrupt North Island concept. "Do not confuse Reinga (the spirit world) with Rarohenga, which is a different place altogether," he said. "It is the place to which Maui went to see his grandfather, and to obtain fire. It is somewhere near where Maui was born . . . towards the east, near Pikipiko-i-whiti." Certainly there are few references in popular mythology to a many-storeyed underworld. On the other hand belief in the progress of the wairua or soul to the Reinga was quite specific and there were many tales about mortals who ventured into the Rarohenga in an attempt to rescue loved ones who had departed from Ao-tu-roa, the world of standing light.

The most interesting and informative of the beliefs about the after-life relate to the journey the wairua made from the place where they were visited by death to the "leaping place."

Towards the point of departure came a never-ending procession of the spirits of the dead. The far north must surely have been crowded with the ghostly, hurrying footsteps of the souls of men. There are weird stories of parties of travellers who have been seen in the distance only to disappear as they came nearer, and then to reappear behind the onlooker. The northern tribes were used to hearing the rustle and movement of countless unseen forms after a battle as the warriors who were killed made their final rendez-

vous in the world of light. It was said that chiefs could be distinguished from slaves. The rangatira passed to one side of a pataka (food store) while the slaves walked underneath. The kumara pits therefore faced north with their backs to the passing wairua lest they enter to make the contents tapu.

At the edge of the long, wind-swept beaches and hills the gales sometimes tied the flax leaves in knots, but according to those who lived there it was the work of the wairua. They left tokens of their passing—leaves of nikau, tree ferns or bracken from those who came from inland parts, dune-grass or seaweed from coastal dwellers.

At the hill Taumata-i-haumu they paused and looked back at the land they had traversed. Here they wept and cut themselves with flakes of obsidian, plucked fresh leaves and wove kopare (mourning chaplets). The hills named Wai-hokimai and Wai-otioti were places for mourning and laceration. Here the wairua stripped off clothes made of wharangi, makuku and horopito leaves. They turned their backs on the world they had loved and, naked as at birth, prepared themselves for the final plunge at Te Reinga.

Some distance south of the Reinga they reached that notable stream Te Wai-ora-a-Tane, the life-giving waters of Tane—surely a sign that they were proceeding from an old to a new life. It was a spiritual Rubicon. Men and women who recovered from severe illness or wounds were said to have returned from the nearer bank of Te Wai-ora-a-Tane. Spirits that came from the east coast had to pass the perils of the Kapo-wairoa Stream at Tom Bowling Bay, where demons endeavoured to seize them as they crossed.

Having reached the rivers of no return on their northern journey the wairua crossed the beach Te One-i-rehi (The Twilight Sands), ascended a slope, and passed over Te Wai-ngunguru (The Water of Lamentation), marching steadily forward to the end of the promontory and the pohutukawa that overhung Te Reinga. It is to be noted that this term was applied not only to the entrance but to the underworld itself. The original pohutukawa was named Aka-ki-te-reinga (Root of the Underworld) and its red blossoms Te Pua-o-te-reinga, which has been poetically rendered as "The Flower of Spirits' Flight."

The wairua waited until the water swirled, displacing the rimu-i-motau (seaweed of Motau) and revealing the entrance, and then dropped into the clear water, into the underworld.

Although some emphasis has been placed on the nether regions as the final abode of spirits—a belief that has its foundation in affection for Papa the Earth Mother and the final embrace of the goddess of death—the Maori also shared the universal Polynesian teaching that the way of the soul led toward the setting sun.

The wairua lingered with the body for the length of time it takes a baby to be freed from its umbilical cord. When it reached the Reinga the wairua dived under the water and came to the surface at Ohau or Manawa-tahi in the Three Kings Islands. On the island a final hill remained to be climbed. Here the wairua chanted its farewell:

> *Ohau i waho ra e—*
> *E puke whakanutuinga*
>
> *Ohau in the distance—*
> *Last hill of farewell*

Thence the way stretched on to the sinking sun, the Ara-whanui-a-Tane (Path laid down by Tane), that lead to far Hawaiki, to Irihia, the Homeland.

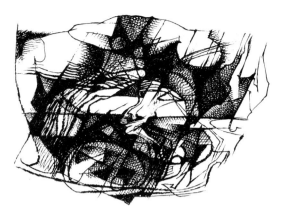

TRIBAL GODS

When internecine warfare spread throughout Aotearoa, the various tribes could no longer claim the exclusive help of Tu-matauenga for help in their feuds. To the powerful departmental deities and other offspring of Rangi and Papa was added a number of tribal atua (gods). They were primarily war gods, though some had peaceful characteristics, being guardians of domestic and agricultural occupations. A few were regarded as more powerful than the others and on account of their prestige such atua were shared by a number of tribes. Prominent among such atua were those who had already won a reputation in Hawaiki and had been "imported" into Aotearoa. Maru, Uenuku, Rongo-mai, Kahu-kura, and Aitu-pawa came in the canoes of the great migration of the fourteenth century. Others were "invented" to become the protagonists of their followers.

Each atua had an aria (manifestation). It is significant that many aria were natural phenomena. The rainbow, thunder and lightning, meteors, comets, and stars doubtless became associated with some important happening in tribal life and so were thought to be the manifestation of a particular god who looked favourably on his tribe or clan. They could then be depended on to provide favourable or unfavourable omens for war parties, and for fishing and bird-hunting expeditions. Not infrequently the atua was in some fashion materialised in the person of a tohunga who interpreted his wishes and warnings.

Maru and Uenuku may be taken to represent the more important tribal atua. None was more widely known and venerated than Maru, a powerful war god noted, amongst other things, for the variety of canoes in which he was supposed to have been brought to Aotearoa. The Taranaki and Whanganui tribes claim that their forbears brought him with them in the *Aotea* canoe and that they offered the first bird taken in the forest to him instead of to Tane. The descendants of *Te Arawa* say that he was brought by Kuiwai and Haungaroa, the sisters of the renowned tohunga Ngatoro-i-rangi, in the *Rewarewa* canoe, while others claim he made the voyage in the *Kurahaupo*. It has been conjectured that he was a voyager of great renown, one whose prowess brought such enduring fame that god-like powers were ascribed to him. His visible form is the red glow that is sometimes seen low on the

horizon and is known as a maru. If it appeared in front of a war party in an undeveloped state it was regarded as an evil omen. The taua would then cancel or postpone the expedition. If the maru was seen behind the war party in an arched form it was regarded as a favourable omen, and the attack would be launched with confidence.

On one notable occasion Maru, together with several companions, went down to the shore where they saw what appeared to be a dead whale lying on the sand, with gulls and flies swarming over it. The atua excavated a huge earth oven, heated the stones, and heaved the huge bulk into the pit.

Unfortunately for Maru and his friends the whale was not dead, and more important still, was not in fact a whale but an unusual form adopted by the even more powerful atua, Rongo-mai. The sleeping god awoke, reared its immense body in the air and crashed down on Maru and the atua who were assisting him. It is evident that this class of atua did not share the immortality of the primal gods for they were all killed. Maru himself, in the form he had adopted at the time, also succumbed—though not his essential spirit. Apparently it was only his material form or manifestation that had been destroyed for Maru rose up to the overworlds and escaped Rongo-mai's wrath by hiding in a fissure in the rocks and from there he continued to influence the tribes who put their faith in him.

Uenuku was the most famous of the atua whose aria was the rainbow, one of his names being Uenuku-tawhana-i-te-rangi (Uenuku-bowlike-in-the-sky), and it is apparent that he was elevated, rather than born, to the status of a god. He was a famous ancestor in Hawaiki, the Homeland, and was deified in New Zealand. There is no record of his being brought in any of the canoes of the migration.

It was in Aotearoa that his full name, Uenuku-tawhana-i-te-rangi, originated, for the reasons given in the following legend.

One morning, before it was light, Uenuku was wandering through the forest and after a time came in sight of a tiny lake he had not seen before. Two personifications who had descended from the sky were bathing there. One was Hine-pukohu-rangi, Girl of the Mist, and Hine-wai, the personification of light rain. After watching for some time Uenuku came to the bank and asked them where they lived.

"We are from Rangi-roa, from Rangi-maomao (the tall sky, the distant sky)," Hine-pukoho-rangi replied.

She turned abruptly to her sister who had been attracted to the handsome young man and seemed inclined to linger.

"Come," she said. "The full light of day is nearly here."

That night Uenuku sat beside the fire in his whare, his thoughts with Hine-pukohu-rangi. The flames died down to a dull glow and the door opened gently. The girl of his dreams stood in the doorway, waiting to be taken into his welcoming arms. They spent the night together and in the morning the young woman joined her sister and left for their home. Night after night Hine-pokohu-rangi returned to Uenuku's whare, but she warned him that he was not on any account to tell his friends of their liaison.

"The time will come, if you are patient," she told him. "When our baby is born you may reveal our relationship. By then I will be ready to live in your world of glaring light. But if you tell them before the baby comes I shall be forced to leave you."

It was difficult for Uenuku to keep silent. He was proud of his heaven-born wife and finally, in an incautious moment, he let fall a hint that was seized upon by the village gossips. They were sceptical and Uenuku was nettled. He soon persuaded himself that no harm could come from revealing the truth. If he was able to show his wife to the villagers then they would know that her beauty was above that of mortal women.

One night he carefully blocked up all the crevices in the walls of the whare to ensure that no light could penetrate the gloom.

At the usual time of waking Hine stirred. "The night is over," she murmured. "I must leave."

"It is still dark. Go back to sleep," Uenuku replied.

Much later she stirred restlessly. "It is a long night," she said. "Are you sure that daylight is not near."

"Yes, the night must be over," Uenuku said. He opened the door. Sunlight flooded the whare.

Hine-pukohu-rangi uttered a cry of distress. She rushed outside, stopped, and looked reproachfully at her husband. Uenuku was standing by the door, with pride in his bearing, as his friends gathered round in a semi-circle uttering exclamations of surprise and approval.

"I did not think you would betray me," she said sadly. She went inside the whare again. Standing under the smoke vent she murmured, "Uenuku! You have shamed me when the morning star appeared and the sun rose. The cry of Hine-wai has not reached me as we lay inside the house. Now I am indeed ashamed in the sight of all your people."

Once again she went through the doorway and rose swiftly to the gable. Uenuku tried to grasp her, but she evaded him. Mist swirled round and hid her from his sight. Like two gauzy clouds Hine-pukohu-rangi and Hine-wai rose into the sky and were never seen again.

In spite of his imprudence Uenuku was deeply in love with his wife and he set out in search of her. Year after year was spent in a vain quest, for he never found the wife of his youth. He grew old and, in a distant country, death at last overtook him. Then the gods took pity on him. They set him in the sky where he became the rainbow that spans the heaven and the atua of fighting men.

In one version of the legend Hine-pukohu-rangi returned temporarily to her home after the birth of her child, named Heheu-rangi, and sang a lament for the child whom she was forced to leave in the world in which she could no longer remain.

There is symbolic significance in the story. Heheu-rangi is the Sky-clearer. Hine-pukohu-rangi's aria can be seen in the rising mist. Hine-wai is the personification of misty rain, and Uenuku the atua who personifies the rainbow.

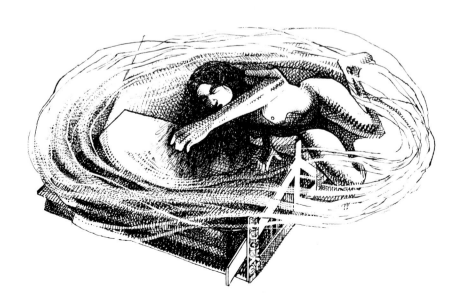

ENCHANTMENT

IN ADDITION TO PERSONIFICATIONS and local atua, the landscape was always liable to invasion by tipua, usually regarded as demons or goblins. The term was frequently used in an adjectival sense and can best be translated as "enchanted". A rakau tipua, for instance, was an enchanted log. Birds, fish, dogs, stones, lakes, mountains, rivers and other objects, animate or inanimate, could under certain circumstances become tipua. The unearthly nature of the tipua was in some cases attributed to the presence of a wairua but this was by no means universal.

Ordinary objects could suffer enchantment and be imbued with unearthly qualities. Some became tipua in a manner that was beyond earthly control; in other cases the enchantment was a result of deliberate action. If the body of a deceased person of some importance was placed at the foot of a tree while the bearer rested, the wairua, or part of the essential essence of the wairua, would attach itself to the tree which would then become tipua. Depositing the umbilical cord of a new born child would have the same effect on a tree or a boulder.

Tipua objects were not tapu nor were they worshipped. They were simply enchanted, and therefore possessed strange powers. The tipua, the demon of the object, needed to be placated by offerings of twigs, sprays, or branches of a living tree. Leaves of the karamu or kawakawa were favoured not only to protect the traveller but also to increase the mana of the tipua. The custom of depositing green offerings was known as uruuruwhenua. The offering was invariably made when the tipua object was first passed and customarily on every subsequent occasion, the surrounding bush often being denuded of foliage.

One notable object to which the offering was made is the stone that sheltered the Rotorua notability Hatupatu when he was pursued by Kurangaituku, the bird-woman. The large boulder by the roadside is a familiar sight to travellers.

Floating logs frequently possessed mysterious powers. Such a log was of great assistance to a young woman who lived on the foothills of the Huiarau Range. Hinerau was famed for her beauty and was courted by young men of noble birth from the surrounding villages. She was gracious to all her suitors but had not found one to whom she could give her heart.

Conscious of her beauty she dressed her hair with care and carried a sachet of sweet-scented moss. The aromatic plants were not easily found and, on one occasion, her search took her far from her home. She lost her way and came unexpectedly to Lake Waikaremoana. Hoping to meet someone who could direct her to her kainga she wandered along the shore. Suddenly the land was shaken by a violent earthquake. The shore was lifted and the lake receded.

Where there had been gently sloping forest land tall cliffs now rose abruptly. The water rushed back, swirling round her, and ebbed again. There was a roar of threshing trees and rumbling landslides, then silence. The ground ceased its movement and Hinerau found that she was confined to a narrow strip of gravel. On every side deep water lapped against the newly-formed cliff face; she was imprisoned on a shelf of rock and gravel.

She lay on the barren shelf throughout the night, shivering with cold and loneliness. When the moon rose she took a sharp-edged shell and scratched through the fibre of a flax leaf until it was severed. then made some marks on it, hoping they would be recognised by one of her lovers who might by this time be searching for her. (It may only be a coincidence that her name has the meaning Leaf Girl.)

Murmuring a prayer to the atua she threw the leaf into the water. Almost immediately she heard unearthly music and in the bright path of moonlight on the lake a rakau tipua drifted toward her. It swept past, caught the flax leaf in its projecting branches, and disappeared into the distance. The music died away. Hinerau's tears dripped on to the rocks and formed a rivulet that grew into a rushing torrent, later known as Te Tangi-o-Hinerau (The Weeping of Hinerau).

Day turned to night and night to day as she sat alone. Suffering hunger she prayed to Rehua for help and the god of kindness, who had once given the tui to Tane, heard her request and sent a flock of kaka. As they circled round she caught one or two of them. Recalling how bird hunters killed them by biting their necks, she also tried to do so, but in spite of her hunger did not have the heart to treat the birds in this way.

Meanwhile the enchanted log had drifted to the other side of the lake. It grounded near the home of the young chief Te Toru, the flax leaf waving like a banner on a branch of the log. The leaf fell into the water and floated to the feet of the chief. Then, to the sound of the weird music, the log went on its way. Te Toru picked up the leaf and in some way was able to construe its message. He launched a small canoe and paddled to the other side of the lake, where he found Hinerau and rescued her.

He took her to wife and she bore him many sons while the wandering log gathered fame as the tipua of Waikaremoana. It seems likely that it was the famous singing log Tutaua that was known to several generations. It had first been placed there by Hau-mapuhia, who formed the lake, and who may herself have been tipua, though she was usually described as a taniwha. The Tuhoe people had a saying they used when they heard its music—Ko Tutaua-e-waiata haera-ana (It is Tutaua singing as it goes.)

The log occasionally drifted ashore. In the course of time it grew malevolent. Whoever touched it was stranded as Hinerau had been, or suffered misfortune in some other way. Finally it disappeared through the outlet at Te Wharawhara, doubtless to the relief of the Tuhoe people. In later years one member of the tribe said, "I myself heard Tutaua, the log demon, singing far out upon the waters, singing in a strange voice like the whistling of the wind."

SYMBOL OF FERTILITY

THE MAURI, THE SUPERNATURAL force that guarded the food supplies of a forest, eel weir, or plantation was jealously guarded. It frequently resided in a stone.

In the forests of Pukekohe the mauri was kept in a secret place on a hillside, its location known only to the ariki of the tribe. The forests were well stocked with kereru, tui, and kaka, and the streams were replete with tuna. The fame of the Pukekohe mauri had spread as far as the Urewera and there a young rangatira of Tuhoe offered to obtain the mauri and bring it to his people, where it would doubtless increase the fertility of the forests of the Urewera.

He left his home burdened with feathered, ornamental cloaks and greenstone ornaments. After a long journey he was made welcome at the large kainga at Pukekohe where, on account of his appearance and ostentatious display of wealth, he attracted the attention of a young woman of high lineage. He courted her assiduously, won her affections, and settled down as a member of his wife's tribe.

The ariki spoke to him one day. He spread his fingers far apart and said, "If you climb the hill over there, and hold up your hand with your fingers wide apart, the kereru will fly down and put their heads between them."

The man of Tuhoe expressed incredulity. The ariki was offended. To maintain the honour of his tribe he offered to demonstrate the power of the mauri on condition that his confidence would not be misplaced.

The two men entered the forest and, as they climbed the hill, they could see the kereru perched on every tree, feeding on the berry-laden branches. When they approached the mauri, the kereru flew down from the trees and put their heads between the chief's fingers.

The young man was still sceptical. "Your mana is greater than that of mine," he admitted, "but that is no proof that your forests yield more than those of my tribe or any other I have seen."

The ariki was startled by the obtuseness of the young man for whom he had some admiration.

"You may have travelled far," he said, "but you have little knowledge. There can be no doubt that the richness of our land is above that of any tribe, nor that any other possesses a mauri of such power."

The Tuhoe rangatira expressed surprise. "You have certainly benefited by the natural richness of land and water, the fame of which I heard even in my home, but unless I see the mauri for myself, and feel its power, whether stick or stone, I certainly cannot believe in it."

The exasperated ariki led the rangatira to an ancient rata tree. In a hollow beneath the trunk lay a round stone. The ariki would not permit him to touch it but even at a distance the young man could sense an aura of tremendous power. Obviously the stone was not light, but it could be carried by a man in one hand.

In the months that followed he kept his promise of secrecy. He told no one of the ariki's indiscretion in showing him the hiding place of the mauri, but his purpose in taking it to his own people was not forgotten.

When the season for replenishing the pataka arrived he took no part in bird-hunting expeditions but joined the eeling parties, often staying out all night, returning late in the morning in order that the people should become accustomed to his being away from home.

One evening he set out early on the pretence of catching eels. He left the cloaks and greenstone ornaments behind as a gift to his wife and those who had befriended him. Lifting the mauri gently from its resting place, he stowed it in the eel basket, and made his way out of the forest.

At daybreak the bird-spearers left the kainga. When they entered the forest they were surprised at the quiet that invaded it. There were no movements in the tree tops, no bird sounds. The silence was oppressive. They summoned the ariki who at once suspected what had happened. He ran to the rata and peered into the hole. As he feared, the mauri was missing.

He summoned a meeting of the kaumatua. No one could offer an explanation until it was reported that the stranger from Tuhoe had set out alone the previous evening and had not returned. There could be no doubt that the ariki's confidence had been misplaced, and that the young rangatira had stolen their mauri.

Two taua were soon on his trail, one travelling on the Waikato River by canoe, the other marching overland. They could detect no sign, however, of the passing of the fugitive who had gone up-river in a small fishing canoe, abandoning it at Taupiri. He had then crossed the swamps to reach the Maungatautari Range.

The stone in his eel bag seemed to grow heavier with every step he took. Looking back from the crest of a hill that had taken toll of his strength he saw his pursuers climbing steadily towards him. They had picked up his trail on leaving the swamps and lacking his heavy burden, were gaining rapidly.

Picking up the basket he had placed on the ground he ran as quickly as he could, heading for Rotorua where he hoped to find shelter. Yet even as the thought of rescue by hereditary enemies of the Pukekohe people entered his mind he realised it was hopeless to try and reach the distant Arawa pa. Already he could hear the thud of feet on the ground and the sound of bodies crashing through the undergrowth. In front of him there was a small lake. Knowing there was no hope of eluding his pursuers, nor of taking the mauri to his own people, he determined that no one else might benefit from the stone and so threw himself over a bluff and sank to the bottom of the lake with the mauri clasped firmly in his arms.

Neither the rangatira of Tuhoe nor the mauri of Pukekohe were ever seen again. The men of the taua returned sadly to their home. As they entered the forest that surrounded the kainga they could see that some of the birds had returned, but they were few in number. The sacred talisman that had attracted them and kept them within the compass of its influence was no longer there and could never be replaced. Pukekohe had lost its reputation as the home ground of all who hunt birds, seek berries, and catch eels. It is said however that the influence of the mauri, emanating from the waters of the lake that concealed it, affected the forests about Rotorua and even extended to the distant Urewera which experienced a rapid growth in its bird population.

MEDIA OF THE GODS

THE TOHUNGA OCCUPIED an important place in the economy of everyday life as well as in the more esoteric elements of Maori thought. Basically he was an expert, whether in the construction of canoes, house building, carving or other occupations.

As the natural and supernatural were so intermingled and interdependent the tohunga was a necessary connecting channel or medium between men and the atua. In order to exercise his functions as a guide to lesser men a word-perfect knowledge of the karakia that ensured the co-operation of the gods was essential. A war party would not dare to set forth on a punitive expedition without a tohunga to interpret the omens that pointed to success.

In this section however we are concerned with the priestly function of the tohunga. The period spent in the whare wananga was long and arduous, no matter what grade of teaching was involved. There were several classes of tohunga ranging from the tohunga ahurewa to the tohunga kehua and amongst them were specialists such as tohunga-tatai-arorangi who interpreted the passage and appearance of the stars, tohunga makutu or whaiwhaia who used the power of black magic to kill, and tohunga matakite who foretold the future.

Within the whare wananga, the school of occult knowledge, the highest class was the whare kura, the school which has already been noted as the home of the baskets of knowledge brought to mankind by Tane. "Black magic" was learnt in an inferior school termed whare maire.

Historical traditions, legends, karakia and the rituals pertaining to war and agriculture were amongst the subjects taught in the whare kura and at the completion of the course, which might occupy several years, tohunga were required to demonstrate their powers by causing green leaves to wither, stones to disintegrate, and birds (and on occasion men) to be killed by the controlled power of the gods.

Although many Pakeha think of the tohunga as "witch doctors", and know something of the way they exercised their power, we must not overlook their influence in government. The priestly function was beneficent. Every action of the tohunga was governed by tapu, the sacredness and strict order of procedure that ensured that men did not unwittingly offend the gods.

The ultimate test of a graduate of the whare maire was his ability to kill a man by the power of mind alone. Lesser men might destroy a dog or a bird but the tohunga whaiwhaia who had gained complete mastery of the powers of makutu was able to project his power over men and women.

A macabre story from the mysterious Urewera country illustrates the depths to which tohunga who dabbled in black magic descended. Kohuru had passed all tests except the final one and he had fallen in love with Titia-i-re-rangi, the daughter of Tawhaki, a tohunga of Urewera. Tawhaki was an adept in the arts of makutu, greatly feared by his people, intolerant and vengeful, and known far and wide as a tohunga whaiwhaia. When Kohuru asked Tawhaki for his daughter in marriage, the old tohunga refused on the grounds that he was immature and unworthy of his daughter.

Kohuru then consulted Tatua-nui, another tohunga of great mana.

"The young hawk may fly further than its parent," Tatua-nui said enigmatically. "Remain with me for three months and we shall see how far you have progressed."

Unaware of the dark heart of the old tohunga and that he had recognised the young man's latent powers and planned to make use of them, Kohuru agreed.

At the end of three months Tatua said, "There is nothing more to teach you. The time has come to put you to the proof. The test will be made at Manukau. I shall go with you to observe the result."

Unfortunately the training he had received had altered Kohuru's nature. Tatua had insisted that tapu must be observed strictly on the journey but Kohuru was not willing to deny himself food and, contrary to Tatua's instructions, he hid a stick freshly cut from a tree and a bundle of fernroot untouched by human hands under his cloak.

Tatua-nui, old and corpulent, found the journey without food or drink a trying experience. Kohuru secretly planted his stick in the ground at each camping place and suspended the fernroot from it so that he could eat without his hands touching it. Although in this way he did not violate tapu he said nothing of his subterfuge to his mentor.

On the third day the old tohunga died of hunger and thirst. With his last breath he urged Kohuru to destroy the chief Matuku who was an old enemy and rival. This in fact had been his purpose in training Kohuru in the deadly arts of makutu.

The young man hastened to Matuku's pa and concealed himself in the fern beneath the palisades. In the cold light of dawn he saw Matuku emerge from his whare and climb the watch tower to see whether any strangers had entered his territory. Kohuru concentrated the powers of darkness in his mind and hurled them at the unsuspecting tohunga. A gleam of triumph flared in his eyes as Matuku jerked and fell backwards.

Kohuru had graduated in the black art with full honours and no longer feared the father of Titia. But on his return to the Urewera Tawhaki was still obdurate.

"Would you accept a tohunga as powerful as Matuku for your son-in-law?" Kohuru asked.

"Yes, there is a man indeed," Tawhaki said.

"Alas," said Kohuru, "he is dead."

"How did he die?" Tawhaki asked in surprise.

"It was I who killed him," Kohuru said proudly. "Look at these. They are proof that I am more powerful than Matuku and more fitted to wed your daughter."

He placed a taiaha, a hei-tiki and a shark's tooth ear pendant that he had taken from Matuku's body in front of Tawhaki.

The older tohunga turned them over and examined them closely. "Yes," he said at last, "these are Matuku's, but what proof have I that it was you who was responsible for his death?"

"These are the proof," Kohuru said impatiently.

"Ah, but I must observe your power for myself before I grant your request. Look, Kohuru. The women are beginning to leave the kumara plantation. They are approaching the pa. Cast your spell on the first one to set foot on the path. If she is dead by the time we reach her I shall give my daughter to you."

They waited until one of the women stepped on to the path. Kohuru concentrated all his powers as he muttered the chant of death and they saw a young woman fall to the ground as Matuku had fallen a few weeks earlier.

Kohuru raced down the path and picked up the body to show Tawhaki that she was dead.

He had indeed triumphed in the dreadful magic of the black art, but he had lost his intended bride as well, for the woman he had killed was Titia-i-te-rangi.

DENIZENS OF THE FOREST

PLEASANT IN ITS sun-dappled freshness, and in the cool depths where the sun seldom penetrated, prolific as a store house of bird life, the bush could in places harbour malevolent creatures that went by names such as patupaiarehe and maero. The latter were the wild men of the forest, ever ready to pounce on unwary travellers. They were found more frequently in the rain forests of the South Island than in the sunnier North Island bush.

The term patupaiarehe, or fairies, which is usually employed as an English equivalent, is far from adequate. They were of more than human height, and fair-skinned. They inhabited the gloomy mist-frequented heights of certain mountains. It is possible that they were a racial memory of fair-skinned people of distant countries. Another theory is that the earliest immigrants to Aotearoa, dispossessed of their lands by late arrivals, took refuge in the bush, building pa on the cloudy summits of the hills and descending from time to time in the concealing mist to abduct and ravish young women. The theory is supported by the belief that diggers of fern-root sometimes heard a mysterious voice that said, "You rejoice today, but my turn will come tomorrow." When the fernroot diggers heard it they set aside the first three roots as an offering to the original inhabitants of the land. Yet another belief was that wairua who had failed to reach the land of spirits were condemned to haunt the forest and hide themselves from the bright light of day. In this respect they had some affinity with kehua, the ghosts who emerged at night to terrify anyone rash enough to venture into the darkness. There is a legend that relates their arrival in the *Taimui* canoe; another that says they were placed in their mountain retreats by the tohunga Ngatoro-i-rangi who came in the *Arawa* canoe. Again it has been said that some patupaiarehe are descended from the atua Tama-o-hoi who divided Ruawahia from Tarawera.

The various branches of the patupaiarehe had certain features and habits in common, though differing in other respects. Being light-haired with fair skin, the urukehu among the Maori regarded themselves as descendants of the patupaiarehe through mixed marriages with mortal women. To a darker-skinned people, the untattooed white-skinned beings were regarded as supernatural. They lived in pa made of the vines of the kareao (supplejack) and ventured far from their pa only on wet or misty days. The plaintive notes of their koauau and putorino exercised a fatal fascination to young women who were lured to the homes of the patupaiarehe. Those who were abducted seldom returned, but lived in a permanently dazed condition amongst their captors.

Fortunately there were two methods of defence against the iwi atua, the supernatural tribe—cooked food and red ochre, which was freely used on tapu objects. The use of these deterrents is illustrated in the legend of Ruarangi and Tawhaitu.

Ruarangi and his young wife lived on the foothills of the Hakarimata Range. Tawhaitu was gathering kumara tubers when her neck was encircled by a strong white arm. She was swept off her feet and carried into the forest.

Wet leaves brushed against her. The mist trailed damp fingers over her face. At the summit of Pirongia the patupaiarehe laid Tawhaitu gently on a bed of moss in one of the whare of the ghostly pa. She lay in his arms throughout the long night listening to the plaintive music of the fairy people and the thin wailing of koauau and putorino while Whanawhana, her abductor and the chief of the hapu, told her of his love. Towards morning she fell into a karakia-induced sleep.

When she woke she found herself lying in a forest clearing near her own home. Her husband Ruarangi was kneeling beside her, looking at her with an anxious expression. He had spent the night searching for her. Hiding her face in his breast she told him how she had been ravished by the dreaded patupaiarehe.

"Whanawhana has laid his evil spell on me," she sobbed. "When it is dark again I shall be drawn to him. I know he has taken my will. I shall not be able to resist his power."

In his distress Ruarangi consulted the tohunga. "There are ways to overcome the patupaiarehe," the tohunga advised him. "You must build a small wharau. Lay a heavy beam across the threshold and paint it with kokowai (red ochre). You must also smear the kokowai over your bodies and your garments.

"When that is done, dig a hole for an umu, light the fire, place food in it, and cover it well. If you do this in the late afternoon the smell of cooking food will last all night long and protect your wife as she lies in the wharau."

That night the slowly steaming umu wafted a savoury smell round the wharau, guarding Ruarangi and Tawhaitu from Whanawhana. Outside the hut stood the tohunga, naked, chanting karakia to repel the patupaiarehe.

Whanawhana and three companions appeared before the wharau. When they attempted to enter they were driven back by the priest's incantations and the smell of cooking food, nor would they have dared to step over the painted beam laid across the doorway. Step by step they retreated slowly to the forest.

Tuwhaitu was not troubled again, though her union with Whanawhana proved fruitful and their descendants, who live by the Waipa River, are noted for the reddish tinge in their hair.

DENIZENS OF THE SEA

THE OCEAN AS WELL as the land was the bride of Rangi. In one account of the creation Rangi the Sky Father married Wainui-atea (Great Expanse of Water), who gave birth to Moana-nui (Great Ocean). The seas were personified in Hine-moana (Ocean Girl), and Wainui (Wide-spreading Water). Not surprisingly Papa the Earth Mother had little love for her rival. In characteristic style Elsdon Best once wrote: "The Ocean Maid is spoken of as constantly assailing the Earth Mother, ever she attacks her; all bays, gulfs, inlets we see are '*te ngaunga a Hinemoana*', the result of the gnawing of Hine-moana into the great body of Tuanuku, our universal mother. This aggression was noted by the Whanau-a-Rangi (Offspring of Rangi), who appointed Rakahore, Hine-tu-a-kirikiri, and Hine-one (personified forms of rock, gravel, and sand) to protect the flanks of the Earth Mother from being swallowed by Hine-moana. When the serried battalions of the Ocean Maid roll in, rank behind rank, to assault the Earth Mother, gaunt Rakahore faces them fearlessly, and they break in fury around him. Still they rush on, in wavering array, to hurl themselves in vain against the rattling armour of the Gravel Maid, or upon the smooth but immovable form of the Sand Maid. They budge not, but ever stand between Papa the Parentless and the fury of Hine-moana."

The origin of the tides is ascribed to Parata, a taniwha that lived far out in the ocean, drawing water in and out of its mouth. By means of the incantations of Ngatoro-i-rangi the *Arawa* canoe was nearly drawn into Te Waha-a-Parata (The Mouth of Parata) but escaped at the last moment.

Nearer to the land the ponaturi, a malevolent marine counterpart of the patupaiarehe, were feared by coast dwellers.

Apart from whales and sharks, some of which have been described as taniwha, and have, on occasion, been well or ill-disposed to mankind, there was a weird creature called marakihau. The carvers of the Bay of Plenty represented it as a figure with human body and head, a fish's tail, and a preposterously long, tubular tongue termed a ngongo. The marakihau was of gigantic proportions, for the tongue was used to draw canoes into its capacious mouth.

Reference has been made several times to transformations and the difficulty of placing supernatural beings into specific categories. Such is the story of Pania and the hairless one.

Pania was a young woman of the sea—not a ponaturi, but with the mind and appearance of a mortal woman. There is no term by which she can be identified.

The land had already exercised a strange fascination for Pania. Every evening she left her home in the sea and lay concealed among the flax bushes at the foot of the Hukarere cliff at Napier, returning to her own people at dawn.

In the half-light of dusk Karitoki, a young chief from a neighbouring village, noticed her as he came to drink the water of a spring. He went over to her, took her by the hand and led her gently to his home. The door closed behind them. Pania was content to remain with this man of the land until the stars grew dim before the dawn light. She left the arms of her sleeping husband, pressed her face gently against his tattooed cheek, and swam through the breakers back to her own people.

Each day as the light waned he waited her coming. Together they made their way past the flax bushes and the spring to their home. As the sea breeze dried her glistening body Karitoki felt the love and the warmth of love welling up and reaching towards him in his strange sea bride.

A year went by. Pania gave birth to a boy, a tiny bundle of humanity she named Moremore (Hairless one). Each morning she left him with her husband. As the chief cared for his son during the day he began to fear that the child might inherit the characteristics of his sea ancestors. He went to the tohunga to ask how he could keep his wife and child with him permanently.

"It should not be difficult," the tohunga assured him, "Wait until they are both asleep. You must then place cooked food on their bodies. They will never return to the sea again."

It was perhaps understandable that the tohunga had assumed that Pania was a ponaturi, or at least had some affinity with these supernatural creatures. The assumption was not correct. In trying to keep his loved ones with him Karitoki lost both son and wife. When she was touched by the tapu-dispelling food Pania took her son in her arms and walked into the sea. She had no wish to leave her husband, but men and women of land and sea have different natures and different customs.

Pania became a rock, which was often frequented by fishermen. In her left armpit the tamure (snapper) swam, and between her thighs the hapuku (groper). Moremore, the hairless one, was transformed into a taniwha. In form he resembled a shark that made its home by the reef off the Hukarere shore and in the inner harbour by the mouth of the Ahuriri River.

In spite of the vast gulf that lies between men and women of alien culture Pania longed as desperately for her lover as Karitoki yearned for her. It is a sad story of lovers parted by conditions over which they had no control. At ebb tide Pania could be seen below the reef with her arms stretched out vainly towards her lover.

DENIZENS OF RIVER AND LAKE

THE FOLKLORE OF AOTEAROA is replete with tales of grisly monsters that inhabited dark caves and pools—a menace to travellers who were unaware of their presence. Monstrous in size as well as form they were called taniwha. Although they were notorious man-eaters many of them could be placated by gifts of food and the reciting of appropriate karakia.

Interestingly there were no reptiles in Polynesia that could have given rise to the concept of crocodile-like monsters, the shape in which they usually appeared. They inhabited salt water as well as fresh, sometimes as sharks, sometimes as whales. The taniwha of the sea were apparently of a more kindly disposition than those of the land. The ocean-dwelling taniwha were known to have rescued shipwrecked and marooned parties and to have escorted sea-going canoes. Whales, which were occasionally designated taniwha, carried men on their backs.

But the vast majority of taniwha had an insatiable appetite for human flesh, even for whole canoe-loads of people. They were descended from the universally-respected god Tane. His daughter Putoto married Taka-aho, Tane's brother, and gave birth to Tua-rangaranga, the progenitor of taniwha. Others, not in this direct line of descent, were believed to be ancestors. Where taniwha were originally human beings, or were inhabited by their wairua, they shared the immortality of the wairua.

It is difficult to know whether to classify taniwha as tipua or atua, especially as the dividing line between the two forms of supernatural beings cannot be determined clearly. There is some evidence to show that they were regarded as atua because, as a learned tohunga once stated, "They dwell as gods on earth, and inhabit the water, inland territory, trees, stones under the earth and in space above." The final phrase refers to flying taniwha, which added a new dimension to the habitat of these monstrous creatures.

One of the more well-disposed taniwha was Horomatangi. He had been brought from Hawaiki by the famous tohunga Ngatoro-i-rangi. After Ngatoro's arrival in Aotearoa his sister Kuiwai was grievously insulted in the homeland by her husband. Together with her sister Haungaroa she came to the new land across the sea in search of Ngatoro to ask him to avenge the insult. The tohunga was unaware of their arrival but the watchful Horomatangi, who at that time was in the vicinity of White Island, saw them.

He then swam under the water until he reached the mainland, travelled underground, and came to the surface of Lake Taupo where he blew a column of water and pumice high into the air, creating a whirlpool some three or four kilometres south of Motutaiko at the Horomatangi Reef. From the lake he saw Kuiwai and Haungaroa in the distance. For some reason the taniwha was unable to reach the women and was forced to communicate with them by signs. Turning and twisting, Horomatangi travelled underground again. At Wairakei he exhaled violently. The earth shuddered as the steam of his breath broke through the ground, forming the Karapiti blow-hole. The white plume of condensing breath gushed high into the air and turned towards Ngatoro's resting place at Maketu. Kuiwai saw the column of steam and interpreted the taniwha's sign correctly.

Exhausted by his labours, Horomatangi remained in the channel between Motutaiko, the little island at the southern end of Lake Taupo, and Wairakei, where he was transformed into a black rock. He sometimes assumes the form of a lizard and is then known as Ihumataotao.

On the nearby promontory of Motutere there once stood an extensive pa, and a church erected more than a hundred years ago. The church had a short length of life. Its early disintegration occurred when a missionary persuaded the inhabitants of the pa to make use of a sacred totara log that floated of its own volition in the neighbourhood of the Horomatangi Reef. The log was either a taniwha or a tipua and may well have been the notable taniwha Horomatangi. When it was hauled ashore and used in the construction of the church its tapu was still potent. The men who cut it up suffered misfortune and the church was soon disused and fell into decay.

Horomatangi also enters into a legend that links Ohinemutu by Lake Rotorua with Rotoaira, the lake that nestles between Tongariro and Pihanga. The taniwha Huru-kareao, who lived in the lake, was a relative of Horomatangi. He had taken the inhabitants of the lakeside pa under his protection and it is said that the men and women of this pa lived lives of such rectitude that Horomatangi was unable to find another hapu of equal reputation. The two taniwha entered into an arrangement to share responsibility for caring for these excellent people.

Having heard good reports of the pleasant springs at Ohinemutu, Hineutu, a young woman who belonged to the Rotoaira hapu, decided to visit the pa by the lakeside at Rotorua. She travelled north and stayed there for a short time. The Arawa people of Ohinemutu heaped indignities upon her, for they had little respect for the southern hapu. They had not heard of the favour with which her people were regarded by the taniwha of Taupo and Rotoaira.

Unable to endure the taunts of the young men and women of Ohinemutu, Hineutu hurried back to her home and called for vengeance. The tohunga chanted incantations to summon Huru-kareao to the pa. The taniwha in turn called his relative from Lake Taupo. When they heard Hineutu's tale their indignation rose to such a pitch that they threw themselves about in the lake, with disastrous results. The pa at Rotoaira was engulfed by the waves. At Tokaanu the surging waters changed the channel of the river and submerged another pa on its banks.

Through Taupo-moana and over the hills and through the valleys the two taniwha sped northwards on their mission of vengeance. They were weary by the time they reached Ohinemutu. They plunged into Lake Rotorua but only half of the village was submerged and many of the inhabitants escaped.

There are three springs, one at Rotoaira, one at Tokaanu, and another at Ohinemutu, all of which are named Huru-kareao. At Motutaiko, Horomatangi lives in an underground cave. For many years he has amused himself by upsetting passing canoes and satisfied his hunger by devouring their crews. Today he lies deep in his cave and contents himself with snapping harmlessly at the propellers of launches, the modern taniwha whose power has outmatched his own.

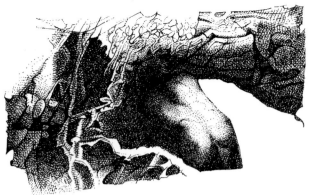

THE COMING OF POUNAMU

As gold to the pakeha, so was greenstone to the Maori. It was intensely hard. It could be ground to a fine edge and was more durable than any other stone. Its translucent colour added beauty to ornaments such as hei-tiki and ear pendants. In this respect it not infrequently served two purposes. A disused adze blade could be fashioned as a tiki. It seems probable that the squat shape with inturned legs and slanted head originated from the shape of an adze head. Possession of tools made of this durable jade was largely responsible for the considerable advance in the art of carving in Aotearoa compared with other Polynesian islands. Greenstone was also an important item of barter between South and North Island tribes. Round its origin and discovery clustered many fabulous legends.

The Maori were convinced that pounamu or greenstone was originally a fish. Captain Cook mentioned this in his journal: "... we were told a hundred fabulous stories about this stone, not one of which carried with it the least probability of truth, though some of their most sensible men would have us believe them. One of these stories is, that this stone is originally a fish, which they strike with a gig in the water, tie a rope to it, and drag it to the shore, to which they fasten it, and it afterwards becomes a stone. As they all agree that it is fished out of a large lake, or collection of waters, the most probable conjecture is, that it is brought from the mountains, and deposited in the water by the torrents. This lake is called by the native *Tavai Poenammoo*; that is, the Water of Green Talc; and it is only the adjoining part of the country, and not the whole southern island of New Zealand, that is known by the name which hath been given to it on my chart."

One of the legends that Cook may have heard is of men who went to the West Coast fiords in search of greenstone. They discovered a large piece in the sea. One canoe took up a position behind it, and one on each side. They drove it southwards along the coast, endeavouring to force it ashore. The fish-like pounamu constantly eluded them. It was not until they reached Bluff that they managed to secure it. The supposed fish-like greenstone is now Motupiu (Dog Island). Local belief was that the island was supported on three greenstone pillars.

To go further back into the mythological past, Poutini was the ancestor of pounamu. Whatu-o-Poutini (Stone of Poutini) and Whatu-o-Tangaroa are poetical terms for greenstone. As the Stone of Tangaroa, god of the sea, its connection with fish become apparent. In one of the several genealogies of Tangaroa, the sea god married Te Anu-matao (The Chilly Cold), who gave birth to four personifications: Pounamu, Poutini, Te Whatukura-a-Tangaroa, and Te Whatu-i-kura, each of whom was a fish.

Poutini was the guardian of Pounamu. In the distant Moana-kura a quarrel arose between Poutini and Tutunui, personification of the whale family. Tutunui wished that the ocean be reserved for his own kindred, fish and shellfish. Poutini demanded that Pounamu be allowed to remain there. It was an irreconcilable difference, for Poutini contended that Pounamu was a fish, while Tutunui maintained that he was merely a stone.

Tutunui enlisted the aid of Hine-tu-a-hoanga, the personification of sandstone and a traditional enemy of Pounamu. As sandstone is the abrasive used in the manufacture of greenstone implements, weapons, and ornaments, the analogy is perfect. Pursued by Hine-tu-a-hoanga, Poutini brought Pounamu to the shores of Aotearoa. A landing was made on Tuhua (Mayor Island). Poutini would have been content to remain there permanently, but Tuhua was the home of two further enemies, Mata (flint or quartz) and Tuhua (obsidian).

Poutini and Pounamu, who may be described collectively as the Greenstone People, fled to East Cape. Here they were opposed by Whaiapu (another form of flint) and Tua-a-hoanga, who appears to be closely related to Hine of that name.

Relentlessly the Greenstone People were pursued and driven from one resting place to another until at last they reached the west coast of the South Island, where they made a determined stand against the Sandstone People.

Pungapunga, the wife of Poutini, was killed. Her name was perpetuated in a light-coloured variety of greenstone. At this point the collective term Greenstone People has become appropriate, for in the battle at Arahura many of their chiefs were captured and taken away as slaves of the Sandstone People. Others took refuge beneath a waterfall, and here, in the river at Arahura, Pounamu took its permanent form as a mother-lode of greenstone.

The waterfall was guarded by a moa which was later killed by the early explorer Ngahue, the companion of Kupe on his epoch-making voyage to New Zealand. As Ngahue is credited with taking moa flesh and greenstone back to Hawaiki, it may be well to include an alternative version of the pounamu legend.

In this tale, Poutini was a block of greenstone that belonged to Ngahue. Whaiapu was a flint owned by Hine-tu-a-hoanga. Hine found it difficult to reduce the unyielding greenstone and drove Ngahue away from Hawaiki. Ngahue arrived at Tuhua with his precious greenstone but, frightened by the appearance of the people who lived there, he made a hasty departure. Traversing the east coast, he became aware of Kanioro "grinding away on the land". Kanioro is a term used to describe the cutting of greenstone by grinding a groove with sand and water. Eventually Ngahue managed to evade his pursuer and took refuge at Arahura, where he broke off a piece to take back to Hawaiki. The famous adzes Tutauru and Hauhau-te-rangi were fashioned from it and, centuries later, were used to fell the trees from which the *Arawa* and other canoes of the Fleet were made.

To complete a trilogy of somewhat confusing and contradictory legends, we introduce Tama-ahua who came from Whangaparaoa and Whangamata in pursuit of his wives, one of whom was Waitaika and who had been abducted by Poutini. Poutini, the pounamu canoe, was afraid of Mata-a-tuhua, the obsidian of Mayor Island, and for this reason had fled southwards.

Tama-ahua used a popular device to discover where his wives had gone. He kept throwing his teka (dart) in front of him and followed it to the place where it fell. The first throw took him to Taupo-moana. The dart kept silent, thus informing Tama-ahua that his wife was not there. The second flight ended at Taranaki, where it crashed against a rock. Tama-ahua then knew that the teka had discovered the path his wife had taken. A further throw and the teka landed at Farewell Spit. Successive casts brought it to Arahura, where Tama-ahua found the sail of the Poutini, which had been wrecked on the inhospitable coast, and knew that his quest was coming to an end.

Tama-ahua made offerings to the atua in the hope that they would restore his wives to life, but his slave had the misfortune to burn his fingers on the cooked food. On licking his fingers to relieve the pain, the tapu was destroyed and the gifts rendered ineffective.

Finally, the legend of Tamatea is told to explain why different kinds of greenstone are found in the South Island. Tamatea-pokai-whenua (or possibly Tame-ki-te-rangi or Tama-ahua) had been deserted by his three wives. He sailed down the east of the South Island in the *Tairea* canoe, rounded the south coast, and went northward until he came to Piopiotahi (Milford Sound). As he searched the shores of the south his clothes were torn to shreds which grew into kiekie and other plants, thus giving rise to a term for vegetation, Te Pokeka-a-Tama (The Rough Cloak of Tama).

At Anita Bay he found one of his wives who had been turned into greenstone. As he bent over her hot tears streamed down his face, dropping into the translucent stone where they can be seen in the type of greenstone known as tangiwai (weeping water). Tangiwai and her children had all been turned into greenstone, but the younger ones had scrambled over the hills and made their home further inland.

Tama left his petrified wife on the beach and went further north until he came to the Arahura River. He travelled up-river until he came to a place where there were many stones and a constant murmur of voices. He did not recognise his other two wives in these enchanted stones, not knowing that their canoe had capsized and that the ledge of greenstone in the river was in reality both the canoe and his petrified wives.

Tama abandoned his canoe and, accompanied by his slave Tumuaki, he stopped to cook some birds. It was here that the slave burnt his fingers and violated tapu, thus preventing any further possibility of bringing the women back to life. Some of the most precious greenstone contains flaws known as tutae koka (excrement of the birds that Tumuaki cooked).

THE COMING OF KUMARA

IN VIEW OF THE widespread cultivation of the succulent tuber known to the Maori as kumara, in the North Island and in the more sheltered districts of the South Island, it is not surprising that a variety of myths was invented to explain its origin.

The kumara was an importation from the tropic Homeland, which fact in turn necessitated a further series of legends to account for its arrival in the southern islands. There are several versions of the manner in which it was brought, one of them concerning Pou-rangahua who lived near the mouth of the Waipaoa river in the days when men lived on the products of lake, river, sea, and forest. It was the craving of Pou's baby son for a mysterious, unknown food that sent the chief far across the Ocean of Kiwa, even to the Homeland, to try to satisfy his child's demands.

At Pari-nui-te-ra his quest succeeded, for there was the site of a famous kumara plantation; but on landing his canoe was wrecked and he had no means of returning to his home. He was compensated for his loss by winning the friendship of the chief Tane, who not only supplied him with an abundant supply of kumara but was also prepared to lend him one of his pet birds, feathered monsters so large and powerful that they were able to carry a grown man on their backs. Pou-rangahua slung two baskets of kumara across the shoulders of one of the birds. It ran quickly along the sand, but under the double load was unable to lift itself from the beach. Tane promptly led forth his favourite bird, the largest and strongest of all, and on its strong back Pou, with the baskets, at last began his flight back to Aotearoa. Skilfully avoiding all the perils of the journey, he arrived safely back at his home.

And so, according to the ancient legend, the kumara came to Aotearoa, the gift from Hawaiki that revolutionised the diet of the Polynesians in this far off land. But Pou-rangahua failed to heed the instructions of his generous host. Though he had been careful to avoid the clutches of Tama-i-waho, the ogre of Hikurangi, on his homeward journey, he was culpably careless of the welfare of Tane's bird when he sent it back to its master.

"Pou returns," he said, "and closes the door for ever."

At Pari-nui-te-ra the Polynesian chief waited in vain for the bird he loved. Aue! Aue! Tired after its long flight and then exhausted by the further flight that Pou had demanded from landfall to home, it had fallen victim to the ogre of Hikurangi.

Other legends relate to a mythical origin, which influenced the elaborate ritual surrounding its cultivation and harvesting. Pani, or Pani-tinaku as she is sometimes known, was the "mother" or personification of the kumara. She was the wife of Rongo-maui, a brother of Whanui; when the star Whanui rose above the horizon, the time had come, said the wise old tohunga, to lift the crop.

Many are the tales that are told of how Pani gave birth to the kumara, tales of how the precious food was stolen from the gods by Rongo-maui and given to the sons of men. It was a heinous theft that robbed the atua of their food and, indeed, it was regarded as the origin of all theft. Whanui looked down at the men and women toiling like ants in their cultivations and in anger sent Anuhe, Toronu, and Moka to destroy the stolen fruits of the earth. It was so then and is still today, for these are the different kinds of caterpillar that feed on the foliage of the tubers.

According to a legend preserved by the tribes of Tuhoe, Pani cared for the five Maui brothers after the death of their parents. One day, when they returned from fishing, they complained to Rongo-maui that he was lazy because he never accompanied them on their fishing expeditions, and failed to help supply the family with food. Rongo resented the criticism. He made up his mind to give them a food supply that would prove he was a better provider than the foster-children of his wife. It was then that he climbed up to the realm of the gods and stole the essence of their food. Descending to earth he impregnated his wife with the seed, the life-spirit of the kumara. When her time came, Rongo told her to go the stream of Mona-ariki to give birth. As she stood in the sacred water she produced her young, the children who were named Nehutai, Patea, Pio, Matatu, Pauarangi, and several others. These are the names of the varieties of kumara provided by that ancestor as food for her descendants.

Then the sacred ovens were prepared, and so men learned the art of cooking food. Had it not been for Rongo-maui, men would be like birds and lizards that eat their food raw.

More than one canoe lays claim to the honour of introducing the kumara to Aotearoa; but it is to Pani-tinaku and her husband Rongo-maui that we render homage for providing mankind with the food of the gods, and to Whanui, the star whose appearance reminds men it is time to harvest the fruits of their labour.

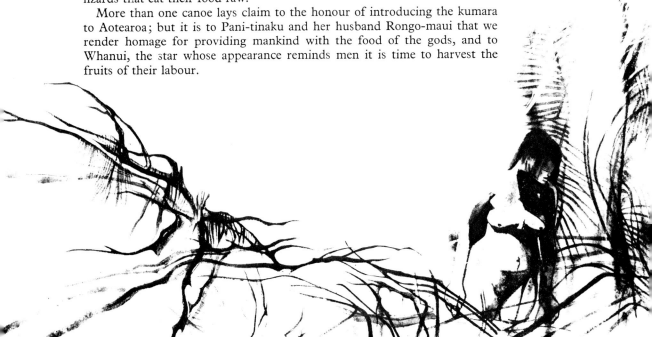

WITCHES AND WARLOCKS

Many tales could be told of unearthly creatures, best described as ogres and ogresses, that do not fit conveniently into any other category. Amongst the most horrifying yet popular tales was that of Ruruhi-kerepo, the old blind woman whose body bristled with bones like a porcupine fish.

Five women left their kainga to walk through the forest. Being young and full of high spirits, they made fun of Ruruhi-kerepo when they met her.

"Look!" one of the girls said. "Here is a ruruhi (old woman)."

"You must never say that to me," Ruruhi-kerepo said.

The girls danced round her, "You are just a Kuia (old woman)."

"Ah," said Ruruhi-kerepo, "I am not really old. Call me matua keke (aunt)."

As the girls quietened down Ruruhi challenged them to see who could climb the highest in a nearby tree. When they were all clinging to the branches she cackled, "Sit there, my nieces. You are lovely girls—so lovely that I could eat you. Each of you would make a tasty mouthful."

She began to shake the branches. The girls saw with dismay that the old woman's hands were strong and hairy with claw-like nails. The nearest girl was shaken off her perch. With a scream she fell into Ruruhi's arms. Opening a mouth that looked like the jaw of a taniwha the old blind woman bit off the girl's head, dropped it on the ground, and swallowed her body whole. One by one the girls were caught, decapitated, and swallowed.

That night there was much speculation as to what had happened to the girls. At first light a party of young men set out in search of them. Suddenly their leader stopped with a look of horror on his face. On the path at his feet lay the heads of the missing girls.

Anger burned fiercely in the breasts of the young men. They spread out and searched diligently through the bush. One of them saw Ruruhi-kerepo. When he came close to her she looked harmless enough so he asked her if she had seen the missing girls. Her gnarled hands shot out and drew him to her. She bit off his head and swallowed his body as she had done with the girls.

His companions saw what had happened. They surrounded Ruruhi. Seeing there was no hope of escape she dropped her cloak to the ground. To their horror and disgust the warriors realised that their clubs would be useless, for the bones of the men and women she had swallowed projected from her body like spines. But death was near. The men drew back and thrust their spears through Ruruhi-kerepo until she bristled with spears as well as bones.

The ogre of Mount Tarawera has the distinction of being described as a maero, an ogre, a tipua, and an atua, and has some of the characteristics of each. Although of ancient ancestry, he is believed to have been alive and active less than a hundred years ago.

Tama-o-hoi was a chief of the tangata whenua, the first people to come to Aotearoa. When later arrivals settled in the thermal regions he frequently left his lair on Mount Tarawera to waylay, kill, and eat unwary travellers. As the victims belonged mainly to the Rotorua and Taupo tribes, Ngatoro-i-rangi, the priest of the *Arawa* canoe, came to their aid. He climbed the mountain and stamped on the summit, which burst open and formed a huge chasm. Then the wise old tohunga thrust Tama into it, closed the opening, and so imprisoned the ogre.

For centuries Tama lay asleep, deep within the mountain, biding his time—until that fateful night in 1886 when the peaks Wahanga and Ruawahia erupted, claiming the lives of many Maori and Pakeha, and scattering boiling mud and ash over the green countryside. The mysterious being who caused the eruption, said many people, was Tama-o-hoi.

The ancient gods have not yet vanished from the land of the Maori for beliefs that are as germane to the land as the vegetation that covers it cannot be completely banished from the mind by the sophistication of modern men. They grow fainter with the passing years until only an irrational fear of kehua (ghosts) comes to the surface when dark shadows move in the bush or round isolated homes or camp fires.

The supernatural has ceased to invade the lives of men, but the shadow of a shadow may yet remain. After the Tarawera eruption Sophia, one of the most celebrated Maori guides, placed on record that "on Tarawera mountain there was a quantity of honey made by the wild bees. No one ought to have touched it, as everything there was tapued; but some young Maori men went up the mountain and took the honey, filling up billies and other vessels with it, and they brought it all away to Te Ariki, and some to Rotomahana, where they gave it to the old chief Rangihehuwa, who lived at the foot of the Pink Terraces. Now I was going to guide my visitors round the Terraces, and when we landed from the boats I saw the old chief Rangihehuwa, and he offered me some of the honey; but I said, 'No, thank you,' for I knew it was tapued; therefore it would be wrong to take it. For had not the two old wise men of the tribe shown me over the mountain where I first came to Tarawera from the Bay of Islands, and did we not see Tamo-o-hoi's cave, and in it his big comb with which he used to comb his hair? It was lying on a stone in the cave. And did not the old men with white hair tell me that everything on Tarawera was tapu? So I had not forgotten their warning, and when Rangihehuwa wanted me to take his honey I said, 'No.' I would not have it or let my people take it either, for I knew the danger, so would have nothing to do with it.

"It is strange but true, every one of those people that ate of the tapued honey, every soul, perished in the eruption of Tarawera, that took place very soon after; but I and my people, who did not touch it, were all saved; and so we came safely and thankfully out of the great disaster of 1886."

GLOSSARY

Aitu-pawa: An atua.
Aka-ki-te-reinga: Root of the underworld.
Anu-matao, Te: Wife of Tangaroa.
Ao-marama: World of light.
Aotearoa: Island of New Zealand.
Ara-whanui-a-Tane: Path laid down by Tane.
Aria: Manifestation of an atua.
Ariki: Chief.
Arohirohi: Personification of mirage.
Atua: God.
Hapu: Sub-tribe.
Hapuku: Groper.
Hau-mapuhia: The taniwha of Waikaremoana.
Haumia-tiketike: God of fernroot and uncultivated food.
Haungaroa: Sister of Ngatoro-i-rangi.
Hawaiki: Homeland of the Maori.
Hei-tiki: Carved neck ornament.
Heheu-rangi: Son of Uenuku and Hine-pukohu-rangi.
Hiku-toia: Fifth underworld.
Hine-ahu-one: The first woman.
Hine-i-tauira: Daughter of Tane and Hine-ahu-one.
Hine-moana: Personification of the ocean.
Hine-nui-te-po: Goddess of night and death.
Hine-one: Personification of sand.
Hine-pukohu-rangi: Personification of mist.
Hine-titama: See *Hine-i-tauira*.
Hine-tu-a-hoanga: Personification of sandstone.
Hine-tu-a-kirikiri: Personification of gravel.
Hine-wai: Personification of misty rain.
Horopito: Pepper tree, *Pseudowintera axillaris.*
Ira atua: Divine element.
Ira tangata: Human element.
Irihia: Original homeland.
Iwi: Tribe.
Kahu-kura: An atua.
Kainga: Unfortified village.
Kaka: Parrot, *Nestor meridionalis.*
Kanioro: Cutting of greenstone.
Karakia: Incantation.
Karamu: Shrub, *Coprosma* species.
Kareao: Supplejack, *Ripogonum scandens.*
Kaumatua: Elder.
Kawakawa: Tree, *Macropiper excelsum.*
Kehua: Ghost.
Kerepo: Blind.
Kereru: New Zealand wood-pigeon, *Hemiphaga novaeseelandiae.*
Kete-aronui: Basket of beneficial knowledge.
Kete-tuatua: Basket of evil magic.
Kete tuauri: Basket of ritual knowledge.
Kiekie: Climbing plant, *Freycinetia banksii.*
Koauau: Flute.
Kokowai: Red ochre.
Kopare: Mourning head wreath.
Kuia: Old woman.
Kuiwai: sister of Ngatoro-i-rangi.
Kumara: Sweet potato, *Ipomoea batatas.*
Kurangaituku: The bird-woman.
Kurawaka: Site of the creation of woman.
Ku-watawata: Guardian of the underworld.
Maero: Wild man of the bush.
Maiki-nui: Personification of great misfortune.
Maiki-roa: Personification of continuous misfortune.
Makuku: Moisture.
Makutu: Witchcraft.
Mana: Influence, prestige.
Marae: Meeting place, court-yard.
Marakihau: Fabulous sea monster.
Ma-rikoriko: Wife of Tiki.
Maru: An atua.
Maru: Glowing patch of sky.
Mata: Personification of flint and quartz.
Matua keke: Aunt.
Maui: A demi-god.
Mauri: Symbol of fertility.
Meto: Tenth and lowest underworld.
Mihi tangata: Wailing of the wairua.
Miru: Goddess of the lowest underworld.
Moana-nui: Son of Rangi and Wainui-atea.
Mumu-hango: Mother of various personifications.
Muri-wai-roa: Part of the underworld.
Ngatoro-i-rangi: Tohunga of *Arawa* canoe.
Ngongo: Tube or mouthpiece.
Nikau: Palm, *Rhopalostylis sapida.*
Pa: Fortified village.
Pa-oro: Echo.
Papa: Earth mother.
Pataka: Food store.
Patupaiarehe: Fairy.
Pikopiko-i-whiti: Direction of the underworlds.
Pounamu: Greenstone.
Pohutukawa: Tree, *Metrosideros* excelsa.
Ponaturi: Sea fairy.

Poutini: Ancestor and personification of greenstone.
Pou-turi: Sixth underworld.
Pu-motomoto: Guardian of the topmost overworld.
Pungapunga: Wife of Poutini.
Putorino: Flute.
Putoto: Daughter of Tane.
Rakahore: Personification of rock.
Rakau: Tree, log.
Rangatira: Person of noble ancestry.
Rangi: Sky Father.
Rangi-maomao: The distant sky.
Rangi-roa: The tall sky.
Rangi-tamaku: Second overworld.
Rarohenga: Underworld.
Rata: Red-flowering forest tree, *Metrosideros robusta and M. umbellata*.
Rawaru: Cod, *Parapercis colias*.
Rehua: God of kindness.
Reinga, Te: Leaping place of wairua.
Rimurimu: Seaweed.
Rohe: Wife of Maui; ferrywoman of the underworld.
Rongo-mai: An atua.
Rongo-ma-tane: God of cultivated food.
Ruruhi: Old woman.
Taheke-roa: Path of the underworlds.
Taiaha: Chief's weapon.
Taka-aho: Brother of Tane.
Tama-o-hoi: An atua or tipua.
Tamure: Snapper, *Chrysophrys auratus*.
Tane: God of forests and fertility.
Tane-mahuta: God of forests.
Tane-mataahi: Creator of birds.
Tane-matua: Creator of trees.
Tangaroa: God of the sea.
Tangata whenua: original inhabitants.
Taniwha: Water monster.
Tapu: Sacred; forbidden; sacred restriction.
Taua: War party.
Tawhiri-matea: God of winds.
Teka: Dart.
Tiki: The first man.

Tipua: Enchanted objects or persons.
Tohu: To guide.
Tohunga: Expert; priest; medium of atua.
Tohunga ahurewa: High-class tohunga.
Tohunga kehua: Lower-class tohunga.
Tohunga makutu: Expert in black magic.
Tohunga matakite: Seer.
Tohunga-tatai-arorangi: Expert in interpreting celestial phenomena.
Tohunga whaiwhaia: Expert in black magic.
Toki: Ninth underworld.
Totara: Forest tree, *Podocarpus totara*.
Tua-rangaranga: Daughter of Putoto and Taka-aho.
Tuha: Personification of obsidian.
Tuhua: Obsidian.
Tui: Parson-bird, *Prosthemadera novaseelandiae*.
Tu-matauenga: God of man and mankind.
Tuna: Eel.
Tutunui: Personification of whales.
Uenuku: An atua.
Uha: Female element.
Umu: Earth oven.
Uranga-o-te-ra: Fourth underworld.
Urukehu: Fair-haired person.
Uruuruwhenua: Offering to an atua.
Wainui: A personification of ocean.
Wainui-atea: Wife of Rangi.
Wai-ora-a-Tane: Life-giving water of Tane.
Wairua: Soul; spirit.
Wananga: Knowledge.
Whaiapu: Personification of flint.
Wharangi: Tree, *Brachyglottis repanda* and *Melicope ternata*.
Wharau: Hut.
Whare: House.
Whare kura: School of learning.
Whare wananga: House of occult knowledge.
Whatukura: Stones of knowledge.
Whatukura-a-Tangaroa: The first whatakura.
Whiro: God of evil.